Grammar Charts for Wheelock's Latin

© Jessica Shao 2014

Wheelock content copyright Martha Wheelock, Deborah Wheelock Taylor, and Richard A. LaFleur; Wheelock's™ is a trademark of Martha Wheelock and Deborah Wheelock Taylor.

The Wheelock's Latin Series is available from HarperCollins Publishers, 195 Broadway, New York, New York 10007, www.harpercollins.com; audio CDs, vocabulary cards, and numerous other ancillaries are available from Bolchazy-Carducci Publishers, Inc., 1570 Baskin Road, Mundelein, Illinois 60060, http://www.bolchazy.com. Teacher's guide, online audio, and other resources at www.wheelockslatin.com.

Chapter 1
Verbs: Present Tense

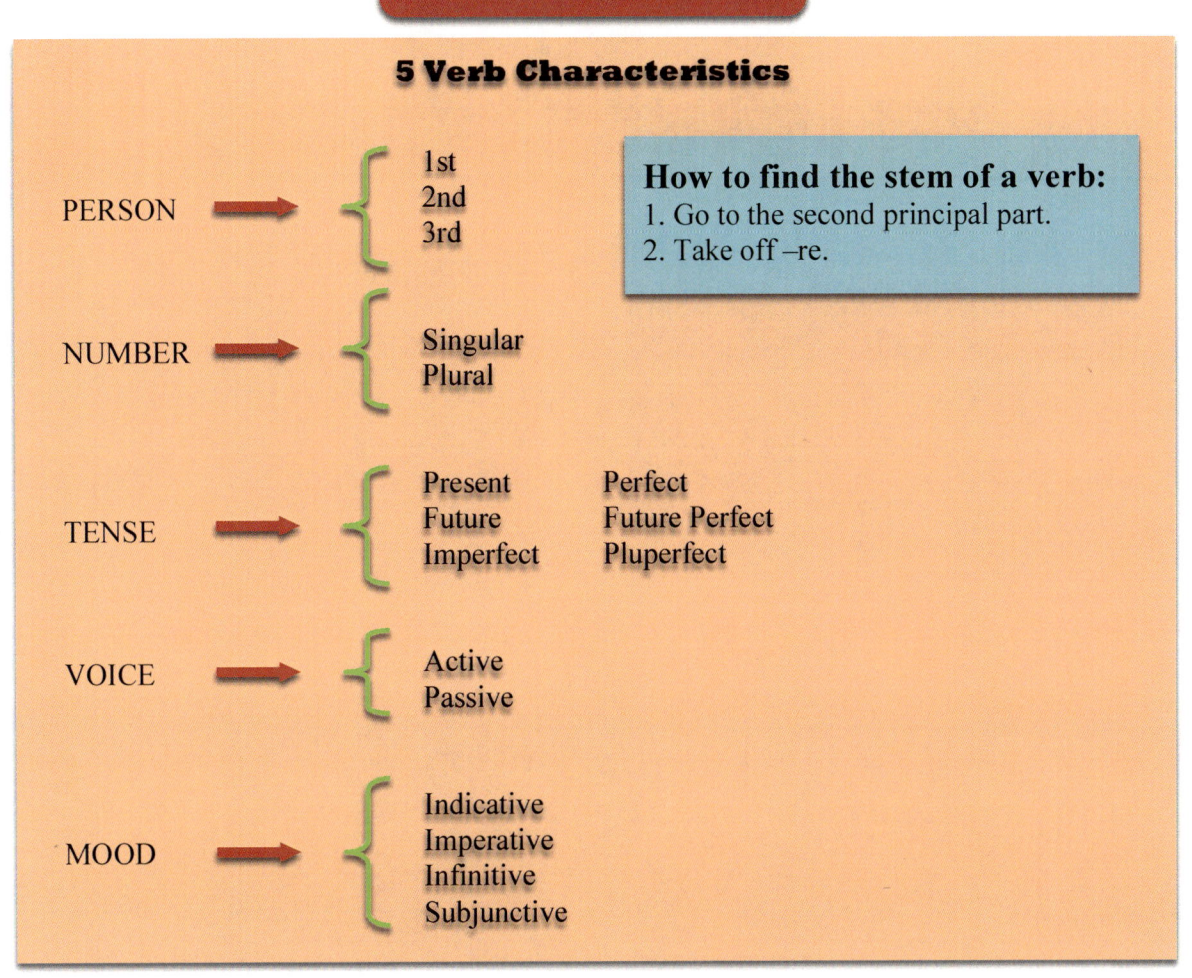

5 Verb Characteristics

PERSON → 1st, 2nd, 3rd

How to find the stem of a verb:
1. Go to the second principal part.
2. Take off –re.

NUMBER → Singular, Plural

TENSE → Present, Future, Imperfect, Perfect, Future Perfect, Pluperfect

VOICE → Active, Passive

MOOD → Indicative, Imperative, Infinitive, Subjunctive

1st and 2nd Conjugations

Present Indicative

	sg	pl
1st	-ō	-mus
2nd	-s	-tis
3rd	-t	-nt

Imperative
Singular: stem
Plural: stem + te

Infinitive
2nd principal part

Chapter 2 Grammar
Nouns and Adjectives: First Declension

6 noun cases:

Nominative – subject
Genitive – possession
Dative – indirect object
Accusative – direct object
Ablative – prepositions or adverbial
Vocative – interjections or address

How to find the stem of a noun:

1. Find the genitive form.
2. Drop the genitive ending.

First Declension

	Singular	Plural
Nom.	a	ae
Gen.	ae	ārum
Dat.	ae	īs
Acc.	am	ās
Abl.	ā	īs
Voc.	a	ae

Chapter 3 Grammar
Second Declension - Masculine

Second Declension
MASCULINE

	Singular	Plural
Nom.	us	ī
Gen.	ī	ōrum
Dat.	ō	īs
Acc.	um	ōs
Abl.	ō	īs
Voc.	e	ī

Chapter 4 Grammar
Second Declension - Neuter

Second Declension
NEUTER

	Singular	Plural
Nom.	um	a
Gen.	ī	ōrum
Dat.	ō	īs
Acc.	um	a
Abl.	ō	īs
Voc.	um	a

Present Tense of *sum* (to be)

	S.	Pl.
1st	sum	sumus
2nd	es	estis
3rd	est	sunt

Chapter 5 Grammar
1st and 2nd Conjugations: Future and Imperfect Tense

Future Tense
"will"

	S.	Pl.
1st	-bō	-bimus
2nd	-bis	-bitis
3rd	-bit	-bunt

Imperfect Tense
"was —ing"

	S.	Pl.
1st	-bam	-bāmus
2nd	-bās	-bātis
3rd	-bat	-bant

Chapter 6 Grammar
Sum and *Possum*

Present Tense of *sum* (to be)

	S.	Pl.
1st	sum	sumus
2nd	es	estis
3rd	est	sunt

Future Tense of *sum* (to be)

	S.	Pl.
1st	erō	erimus
2nd	eris	eritis
3rd	erit	erunt

Imperfect Tense of *sum* (to be)

	S.	Pl.
1st	eram	erāmus
2nd	erās	erātis
3rd	erat	erant

possum, posse, potuī (to be able, can)

1. Add the prefix *pot-* to a form of the verb *sum*.

2. If the form of *sum* begins with an "s", change *pot-* to *pos-* (e.g. *possum*)

Chapter 7 Grammar
Third Declension

Third Declension
All Genders

Singular

	Masc. & Fem.	Neuter
Nom.	--	--
Gen.	-is	-is
Dat.	-ī	-ī
Acc.	-em	--
Abl.	-e	-e

Plural

	Masc. & Fem.	Neuter
Nom.	-ēs	-a
Gen.	-um	-um
Dat.	-ibus	-ibus
Acc.	-ēs	-a
Abl.	-ibus	-ibus

Chapter 8 Grammar
Third Conjugation

Present Tense

	S.	Pl.
1st	-ō	-imus
2nd	-is	-itis
3rd	-it	-unt

Future Tense

	S.	Pl.
1st	-am	-ēmus
2nd	-ēs	-ētis
3rd	et	-ent

Imperfect Tense

	S.	Pl.
1st	-ēbam	-ēbāmus
2nd	-ēbās	-ēbātis
3rd	-ēbat	-ēbant

Finding the Stem

1. Go to the 2nd principal part.
2. Drop off *-ere*.

Example: agō, **ag**ere, ēgī, āctum

Imperatives

Singular: ag**e**
Plural: ag**ite**

Chapter 9 Grammar
Demonstratives; "UNUS NAUTA" Adjectives

ille: *that, those*

Singular

	Masc.	Fem.	Neut.
Nom.	ille	illa	illud
Gen.	illīus	illīus	illīus
Dat.	illī	illī	illī
Acc.	illum	illam	illud
Abl.	illō	illā	illō

Plural

	Masc.	Fem.	Neut.
Nom.	illī	illae	illa
Gen.	illōrum	illārum	illōrum
Dat.	illīs	illīs	illīs
Acc.	illōs	illās	illa
Abl.	illīs	illīs	illīs

hic: *this, these*

Singular

	Masc.	Fem.	Neut.
Nom.	hic	haec	hoc
Gen.	huius	huius	huius
Dat.	huic	huic	huic
Acc.	hunc	hanc	hoc
Abl.	hōc	hāc	hōc

Plural

	Masc.	Fem.	Neut.
Nom.	hī	hae	haec
Gen.	hōrum	hārum	hōrum
Dat.	hīs	hīs	hīs
Acc.	hōs	hās	haec
Abl.	hīs	hīs	hīs

Iste, ista, istud, *that of yours, that,* is declined like *ille*.

Special "-ius" Adjectives: Decline singular genitives and datives like *ille*.

Ūnus, -a, -um: *one*
Nūllus, -a, -um: *no, none*
Ūllus, -a, -um: *any*
Sōlus, -a, -um: *alone, only*

Neuter, neutra, neutrum: *neither*
Alius, -a, -ud: *another, other*
Uter, utra, utrum: *either*
Tōtus, -a, -um: *whole, entire*
Alter, altera, alterum: *the other (of two)*

Chapter 10 Grammar
Fourth Conjugation; Third Conjugation –iō

4TH CONJUGATION

Present Tense

	S.	Pl.
1st	-ō	-mus
2nd	-s	-tis
3rd	-t	-(u)nt

Future Tense

	S.	Pl.
1st	-am	-ēmus
2nd	-ēs	-ētis
3rd	et	-ent

Imperfect Tense

	S.	Pl.
1st	-ēbam	-ēbāmus
2nd	-ēbās	-ēbātis
3rd	-ēbat	-ēbant

*The stem vowel -i- precedes all the above endings and is long only in *audīs*, *audīmus*, and *audītis*.

3RD CONJUGATION -iō

Present Tense

	S.	Pl.
1st	-ō	-mus
2nd	-s	-tis
3rd	-t	-(u)nt

Future Tense

	S.	Pl.
1st	-am	-ēmus
2nd	-ēs	-ētis
3rd	et	-ent

Imperfect Tense

	S.	Pl.
1st	-ēbam	-ēbāmus
2nd	-ēbās	-ēbātis
3rd	-ēbat	-ēbant

*short -i- precedes all the above endings

Finding the Stem
1. Go to the 2nd principal part.
2. Drop off *-re*.

Example: audiō, audīre, audīvī, audītum

Imperatives
Singular: stem
Plural: stem + **te** (3rd –iō: stem + **ite**)

Chapter 11 Grammar
Personal Pronouns
The Demonstrative *Īdem*

First Person

Singular

N.	ego
G.	meī
D.	mihi
A.	mē
Ab.	mē

Plural

N.	nōs
G.	nostrum/nostrī
D.	nōbīs
A.	nōs
Ab.	nōbīs

Second Person

Singular

N.	tū
G.	tuī
D.	tibi
A.	tē
Ab.	tē

Plural

N.	vōs
G.	vestrum/vestrī
D.	vōbīs
A.	vōs
Ab.	vōbīs

Third Person

Singular

	Masc.	Fem.	Neut.
N.	is	ea	id
G.	eius	eius	eius
D.	eī	eī	eī
A.	eum	eam	id
Ab.	eō	eā	eō

Plural

	Masc.	Fem.	Neut.
N.	eī/iī	eae	ea
G.	eōrum	eārum	eōrum
D.	eīs	eīs	eīs
A.	eōs	eās	ea
Ab.	eīs	eīs	eīs

The **Demonstrative** *īdem, eadem, idem* is formed by adding *–dem* directly to the forms of *is, ea, id*.

Note the following 8 exceptions:
Nominative singulars: *īdem, (eadem), idem*
Accusative singulars: *eundem, eandem, idem*
Genitive plurals: *eōrundem, eārundem, eōrundem*

Chapter 12 Grammar
The Perfect Active System

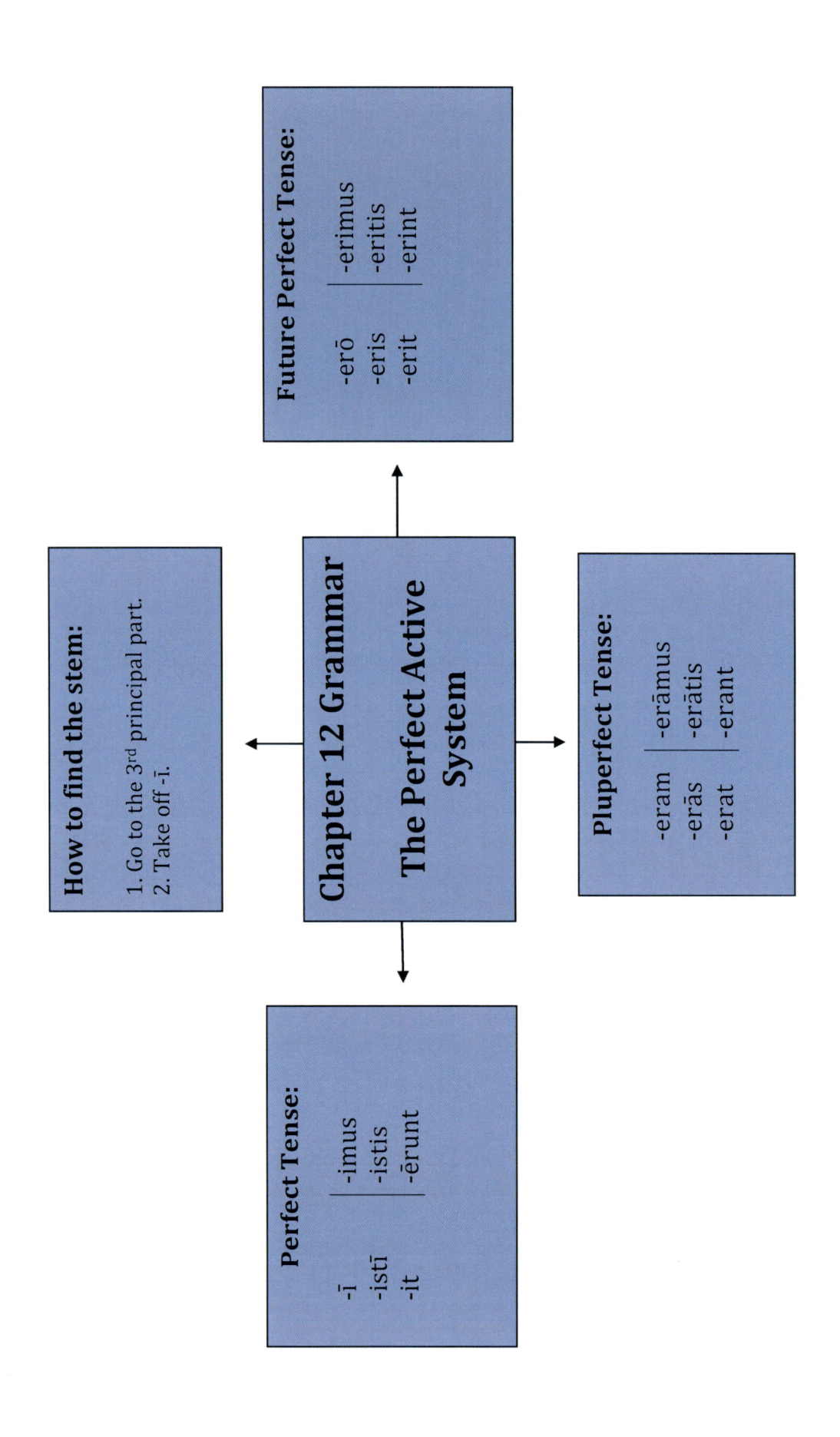

How to find the stem:
1. Go to the 3rd principal part.
2. Take off -ī.

Future Perfect Tense:

-erō   -erimus
-eris   -eritis
-erit   -erint

Pluperfect Tense:

-eram   -erāmus
-erās   -erātis
-erat   -erant

Perfect Tense:

-ī   -imus
-istī   -istis
-it   -ērunt

Chapter 13 Grammar

Reflexive Pronouns
Reflexive Possessives
Intensive Pronouns

Reflexive Pronouns:

	1st person	2nd person	3rd person
N	-----	-----	-----
G	meī	tuī	suī
D	mihi	tibi	sibi
A	mē	tē	sē
Ab	mē	tē	sē
N	-----	-----	-----
G	nostrī	vestrī	suī
D	nōbīs	vōbīs	sibi
A	nōs	vōs	sē
Ab	nōbīs	vōbis	sē

Intensive Pronouns:

	Masc.	Fem.	Neut.
N	ipse	ipsa	ipsum
G	ipsīus	ipsīus	ipsīus
D	ipsī	ipsī	ipsī
A	ipsum	ipsam	ipsum
Ab	ipsō	ipsā	ipsō
N	ipsī	ipsae	ipsa
G	ipsōrum	ipsārum	ipsōrum
D	ipsīs	ipsīs	ipsīs
A	ipsōs	ipsās	ipsa
Ab	ipsīs	ipsīs	ipsīs

Reflexive Possessives are adjectives.

Rules:
1. Must agree with the noun it modifies in gender, number, and case.
2. In translation only, the gender and number must match the subject.

	1st person	2nd person	3rd person
Singular	meus, mea, meum	tuus, tua, tuum	suus, sua, suum
Plural	noster, nostra, nostrum	vester, vestra, vestrum	suī, suae, sua

Chapter 14 Grammar
I-Stem Nouns
Ablatives

Recognizing I-Stem Nouns

Characteristics of group 1:
- Masculine or Feminine
- Nominative singular ends in **-is** or **-ēs**
- Nom. and Gen. have the same number of syllables
- Examples: *hostis, hostis; molēs, molis*

Characteristics of group 2:
- Masculine or Feminine
- Nominative singular ends in **-s** or **-x**
- Stem ends with two consonants
- Examples: *ars, artis; nox, noctis*

Characteristics of group 3:
- Neuter
- Nominative singular ends in **-al, -ar, -e**
- Examples: *animal, animālis; mare, maris*

Declining I-Stem Nouns

I-Stem nouns are *third declension* nouns. There are only a few new endings.

All nouns:
- Genitive plural **-ium**

Only neuter nouns:
- Ablative singular **-ī**
- Nom/Acc plural **-ia**

Types of Ablatives

1) Ablative of Means (no preposition) – answers the question "by means of what?"

2) Ablative of Manner (*cum* + abl.) – answers the question "how?"

3) Ablative of Accompaniment (*cum* + abl.) – answers the question "with whom?"

Chapter 15 Grammar
Numerals
Ablatives and Genitives

duo, two

	M.	F.	N.
N.	duo	duae	duo
G.	duōrum	duārum	duōrum
D.	duōbus	duābus	duōbus
A.	duōs	duās	duo
Ab.	duōbus	duābus	duōbus

tres, three

	M. F.	N.
N.	trēs	tria
G.	trium	trium
D.	tribus	tribus
A.	trēs	tria
Ab.	tribus	tribus

mille, thousand

	M. F. N.	N. Pl.
N.	mīlle	mīlia
G.	mīlle	mīlium
D.	mīlle	mīlibus
A.	mīlle	mīlia

Types of Ablatives

4) Ablative of Time When or Within Which (no preposition): introduced with the words *at, on, in, within*

Types of Genitives

1) Partitive Genitive: indicates the whole of some thing or group after a word designating a part (also called Genitive of the Whole)

Chapter 16 Grammar
Third Declension Adjectives

How to decline:
Same as I-Stem nouns (see Ch. 14)
Rules for 3rd declension adjectives:
1. **–ī** in the ablative singular of ALL genders (not just neuter)
2. **–ium** in the genitive plural
3. **–ia** in the nom. and acc. plural of the neuter

3-ending adjectives:
- example: *ācer, ācris, ācre*
- Nominatives of all three genders are given.

2-ending adjectives
- example: *fortis, forte*
- Nominative forms are given.
- The first form is both masculine AND feminine.
- The second form is neuter.

1-ending adjectives
- example: *potēns, potentis*
- Nominative and genitive forms are given.
- Same nominative form for ALL genders.

Chapter 17 Grammar
The Relative Pronoun

quī, quae, quod, *who, which, that*

Sing.	M.	F.	N.
N.	quī	quae	quod
G.	cuius	cuius	cuius
D.	cui	cui	cui
A.	quem	quam	quod
Ab.	quō	quā	quō

Plur.	M.	F.	N.
N.	quī	quae	quae
G.	quōrum	quārum	quōrum
D.	quibus	quibus	quibus
A.	quōs	quās	quae
Ab.	quibus	quibus	quibus

Agreement

Remember that a relative pronoun must agree with its ANTECEDENT in gender and number, but its CASE depends upon its use in its own clause.

Chapter 18 Grammar
Passive Voice (1st and 2nd conjugations)
Ablative of Agent

1st and 2nd conjugations

Present Tense

	sing.	plur.
1st	-or	-mur
2nd	-ris	-minī
3rd	-tur	-ntur

Future Tense

	sing.	plur.
1st	-bor	-bimur
2nd	-beris	-biminī
3rd	-bitur	-buntur

Imperfect Tense

	sing.	plur.
1st	-bar	-bāmur
2nd	-bāris	-bāminī
3rd	-bātur	-bantur

Passive Infinitive
Take 2nd principal part.
Change the last **-e** to an **-ī**.
(e.g. *laudāre* → *laudārī*)

Types of Ablatives
5) Ablative of Personal Agent (with *ab*)
   Answers the question: By whom?
   (*ab* + ablative)

Chapter 19 Grammar
Perfect Passive System
Interrogative Pronouns
Interrogative Adjectives

Perfect Passive System

Perfect Tense
4th principal part + present tense "to be"

Future Perfect Tense
4th principal part + future tense "to be"

Pluperfect Tense
4th principal part + imperfect tense "to be"

The Interrogative Pronoun (who? what?)

M/F	N	M. Plural	F. Plural	N. Plural
quis	quid	quī	quae	quae
cuius	cuius	quōrum	quārum	quōrum
cui	cui	quibus	quibus	quibus
quem	quid	quōs	quās	quae
quō	quō	quibus	quibus	quibus

The Interrogative Adjective (which?)

The interrogative adjective has forms identical to those of the relative pronoun but precedes a noun in the same gender, number, and case.

e.g. *quae discipula*, which student?

Chapter 20 Grammar
Fourth Declension
More Ablatives

Fourth Declension

SINGULAR	M. and F.	N.
Nom.	-us	-ū
Gen.	-ūs	-ūs
Dat.	-uī	-ū
Acc.	-um	-ū
Abl.	-ū	-ū

PLURAL		
Nom.	-ūs	-ua
Gen.	-uum	-uum
Dat.	-ibus	-ibus
Acc.	-ūs	-ua
Abl.	-ibus	-ibus

Types of Ablatives

6) Place from Which – Active motion from one place to another; usually accompanied by **ab**, **dē**, or **ex**

7) Separation – Person or thing separated from another; may or may not have a preposition

Chapter 21 Grammar
Passive Voice (3rd and 4th conj.)

3rd conjugation

Present Tense

	sing.	plur.
1st	-or	-imur
2nd	-eris	-iminī
3rd	-itur	-untur

Future Tense

	sing.	plur.
1st	-ar	-ēmur
2nd	-ēris	-ēminī
3rd	-ētur	-entur

Imperfect Tense

	sing.	plur.
1st	-ēbar	-ēbāmur
2nd	-ēbāris	-ēbāminī
3rd	-ēbātur	-ēbantur

4th conjugation

Present Tense

	sing.	plur.
1st	-or	-mur
2nd	-ris	-minī
3rd	-tur	-untur

Future Tense

	sing.	plur.
1st	-ar	-ēmur
2nd	-ēris	-ēminī
3rd	-ētur	-entur

Imperfect Tense

	sing.	plur.
1st	-ēbar	-ēbāmur
2nd	-ēbāris	-ēbāminī
3rd	-ēbātur	-ēbantur

Passive Infinitive

3rd conjugation:
　　Take the 2nd principal part.
　　Drop –ere.
　　Add an -ī.
　　(e.g. *agere* →*agī*)

4th conjugation:
　　Take 2nd principal part.
　　Change the last -e to an -ī.
　　(e.g. *audīre* →*audīrī*)

3rd –iō conjugation

Add a short -i- to the stem then use 4th conjugation endings.
(e.g. *capior*)

Only exception: the 2nd person singular, present tense ending is –**eris**. (e.g. *caperis*)

Chapter 22 Grammar
Fifth Declension
More Ablatives

Fifth Declension

SINGULAR	F.	*diēs, diēī*
Nom.	-ēs	-ēs
Gen.	-eī	**-ēī**
Dat.	-eī	**-ēī**
Acc.	-em	-em
Abl.	-ē	-ē
PLURAL		
Nom.	-ēs	-ēs
Gen.	-ērum	-ērum
Dat.	-ēbus	-ēbus
Acc.	-ēs	-ēs
Abl.	-ēbus	-ēbus

Types of Ablatives

8) Place Where – Indicates where something takes place; often with **in** or **sub**

Chapter 23 Grammar
Parciples

Forming Participles

	Active	Passive
Pres.	Present stem + **-ns, -ntis**	------
Perf.	------	Participial stem + **-us, -a, -um**
Fut.	Participial stem + **-ūrus, -ūra, -ūrum**	Present stem + **-ndus, -nda, -ndum**

Example with the verb: agō, agere, ēgī, āctum *(to lead)*

	Active	Passive
Pres.	agēns, agentis *(leading)*	------
Perf.	------	āctus, -a, -um *(having been led)*
Fut.	āctūrus, -a, -um *(about to lead)*	agendus, -a, -um *(about to be led)*

Chapter 24 Grammar
Ablative Absolute
Passive Periphrastic

Ablative Absolute

1. A phrase loosely connected to the main clause.

2. The phrase contains a noun and participle in the **ablative** case.

Passive Periphrastic with Dative of Agent

1. The future passive participle **agrees with its subject** in gender, number, and case.

2. Indicates necessary, obligatory, or appropriate action.

3. When the construction expresses the person who should perform the action, the agent is in the **dative case** (not the ablative of agent).

Chapter 25 Grammar
Infinitives
Indirect Statements

Infinitives

	Active	Passive
Pres.	-āre, -ēre, -ere, -īre	-ārī, -ērī, -ī, -īrī
Perf.	perfect stem + **-isse**	perfect passive participle + **esse**
Fut.	future active participle + **esse**	(supine in **–um + īrī**)

Indirect Statements:
Identifying and Translating

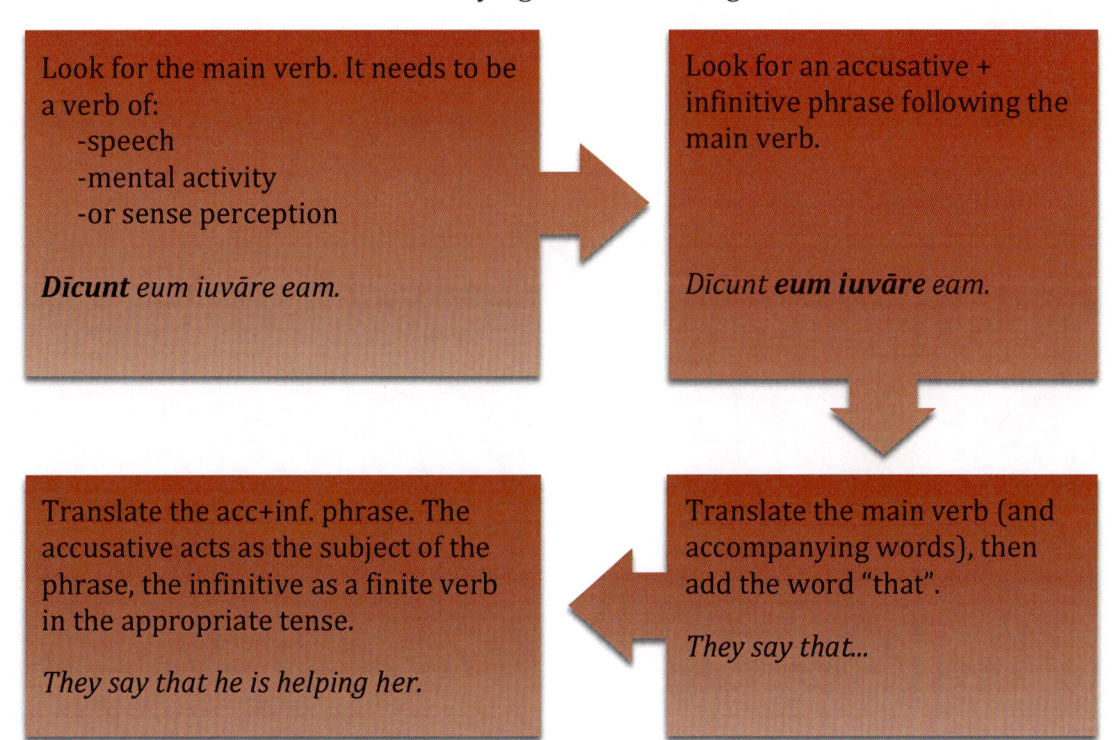

Look for the main verb. It needs to be a verb of:
- speech
- mental activity
- or sense perception

Dīcunt eum iuvāre eam.

→

Look for an accusative + infinitive phrase following the main verb.

*Dīcunt **eum iuvāre** eam.*

↓

Translate the acc+inf. phrase. The accusative acts as the subject of the phrase, the infinitive as a finite verb in the appropriate tense.

They say that he is helping her.

←

Translate the main verb (and accompanying words), then add the word "that".

They say that...

Chapter 26 Grammar
Comparison of Adjectives
Ablative of Comparison

Comparison of Adjectives Forms

Positive: dictionary form

Declined like *magnus-a-um*

Comparative: base of positive + **-ior, -iōris** (neuter: **-ius, -iōris**)

Declined like 3rd declension adjectives with 2 endings

Superlative: base of positive + **-issimus, -issima, -issimum**

Declined like *magnus-a-um*

Ablative of Comparison

Used with comparative adjectives as the second object of comparison.

It is a noun in the ablative case without a preposition.

Example:

I have seen few men happier **than your father**.

*Vīdī paucōs fēlīciōrēs **patre tuō***.

Chapter 27 Grammar
Special and Irregular Comparison of Adjectives

Irregular Adjectives

Positive	Comparative	Superlative
bonus, -a, -um (good)	melior, -ius (better)	optimus, -a, -um (best)
magnus, -a, -um (great)	maior, -ius (greater)	maximus, -a, -um (greatest)
malus, -a, -um (bad)	peior, -ius (worse)	pessimus, -a, -um (worst)
multus, -a, -um (much)	*see chart below* (more)	plūrimus, -a, -um (most)
parvus, -a, -um (small)	minor, minus (smaller)	minimus, -a, -um (smallest)
(prae, prō) (in front of, before)	prior, -ius (former)	prīmus, -a, -um (first)
superus, -a, -um (above)	superior, -ius (higher)	summus, -a, -um (highest, furthest) suprēmus, -a, -um (highest, last)

Special Superlatives

1. Six –lis adjectives add *-limus, -lima, -limum* to the stem
   i. facilis > facillimus, -a, -um
   ii. difficilis
   iii. similis
   iv. dissimilis
   v. gracilis
   vi. humilis

2. All adjectives ending with -er use *-rimus, -rima, -rimum*.
   i. Add the ending to the masculine nominative form
   ii. e.g. *pulcher > pulcherrimus*

Declension of *plūs*

Singular N.	Plural M. & F.	Plural N.
plūs	plūrēs	plūra
plūris	plūrium	plūrium
------	plūribus	plūribus
plūs	plūrēs	plūra
plūre	plūribus	plūribus

Chapters 28-30 Grammar
The Subjunctive Mood

PRESENT

ACTIVE
- Take root
- Change stem vowel to **wE fEAr A lIAr**
- Add present endings

Examples
1. laud**e**m
2. mon**ea**m
3. ag**a**m
4. aud**ia**m
3-iō. cap**ia**m

PASSIVE
- Same as active
- Change personal endings to:
  -r
  -ris
  -tur
  -mur
  -minī
  -ntur

Examples
1. lauder
2. monear
3. agar
4. audiar
3-iō. capiar

IMPERFECT

ACTIVE
- Take **present active infinitive**
- Add present endings

Examples
1. laudārem
2. monērem
3. agerem
4. audīrem
3-iō. caperem

PASSIVE
- Same as active
- Change endings to passive

Examples
1. laudārer
2. monērer
3. agerer
4. audīrer
3-iō. caperer

PERFECT

ACTIVE
- Take **perfect stem**
- Add **-ERI-**
- Add present endings

Examples
1. laudāverim
2. monuerim
3. ēgerim
4. audīverim
3-iō. cēperim

PASSIVE
- Take **perfect passive participle**
- Add **present subjunctive** of sum

Examples
1. laudātus sim
2. monitus sim
3. āctus sim
4. audītus sim
3-iō. captus sum

PLUPERFECT

ACTIVE
- Take **perfect active infinitive**
- Add present endings

Examples
1. laudāvissem
2. monuissem
3. ēgissem
4. audīvissem
3-iō. cepissem

Passive
- Take **perfect passive participle**
- Add **imperfect subjunctive** of sum

Examples
1. laudātus essem
2. monitus essem
3. āctus essem
4. audītus essem
3-iō. captus essem

Subjunctive of *SUM* and *POSSUM*

Present Subjunctive		Imperfect Subjunctive	
sim	possim	essem	possem
sīs	possīs	essēs	possēs
sit	possit	esset	posset
sīmus	possīmus	essēmus	possēmus
sītis	possītis	essētis	possētis
sint	possint	essent	possent

Chapter 31 Grammar
Irregular Verb: *Ferō*

All other tenses are formed like regular 3rd conjugation verbs.

Present Indicative Active	Present Indicative Passive
ferō	feror
fers	ferris
fert	fertur
ferimus	ferimur
fertis	feriminī
ferunt	feruntur

Present Imperative Active
fer, ferte

Infinitive Active	Infinitive Passive
Pres. ferre	Pres. ferrī
Perf. tulisse	Perf. lātus esse
Fut. lātūrus esse	Fut. lātum īrī

Chapter 32 Grammar
Comparison of Adverbs
Volō, Nōlō, Mālō

Formation of Adverbs

Positive: base of positive adjective + **-ē** (+ **-iter** for 3rd decl.)

Comparative: neuter comparative adjective (ends in **-ius**)

Superlative: superlative adjective with the ending **-e**

Irregular Adverbs

Positive	Comparative	Superlative
bene (well)	**melius** (better)	**optimē** (best)
male (badly)	**peius** (worse)	**pessimē** (worst)
multum (much)	**plūs** (more, *quantity*)	**plūrimum** (most, very much)
magnopere (greatly)	**magis** (more, *quality*)	**maximē** (most, especially)
(pro)	**prius** (before, earlier)	**prīmō/prīmum** (at first/in the first place)
diū (for a long time)	**diūtius** (longer)	**diūtissimē** (very long)

volō, velle, voluī

Pres. Ind.	Pres. Subj.
volō	velim
vīs	velīs
vult	velit
volumus	velīmus
vultis	velītis
volunt	velint

nōlō, nōlle, nōluī

Pres. Ind.	Pres. Subj.
nōlō	nōlim
nōn vīs	nōlīs
nōn vult	nōlit
nōlumus	nōlīmus
nōn vultis	nōlītis
nōlunt	nōlint

mālō, mālle, māluī

Pres. Ind.	Pres. Subj.
mālo	mālim
māvīs	mālīs
māvult	mālit
mālumus	mālīmus
māvultis	mālītis
mālunt	mālint

Chapter 33 Grammar
Conditional Sentences

Conditional Type	Protasis Tense	Apodosis Tense	How to Translate	Example
Present Simple	Present	Present	Present → Present	If she is thinking this, she is wise. *Sī id putat, prūdēns est.*
Past Simple	Perfect/Imperfect	Perfect/Imperfect	Past → Past	If she thought this, she was wise. *Sī id putāvit, prūdēns fuit.*
Future More Vivid	Future	Future	Present → Future	If she thinks this, she will be wise. *Sī id putābit, prūdēns erit.*
Present Contrafactual	Imperfect Subjunctive	Imperfect Subjunctive	were → would	If she were thinking this, she would be wise. *Sī id putāret, prūdēns esset.*
Past Contrafactual	Pluperfect Subjunctive	Pluperfect Subjunctive	had → would have	If she had thought this, she would have been wise. *Sī id putāvisset, prūdēns fuisset.*
Future Less Vivid	Present Subjunctive	Present Subjunctive	should → would	If she should think this, she would be wise. *Sī id putet, prūdēns sit.*

Chapter 34 Grammar
Deponent Verbs
Ablatives with Special Deponents

How to Conjugate Deponents

Indicatives: Use regular passive voice endings

Subjunctives: Use regular passive voice endings

Infinitives:

　　Present: -ārī, -ērī, -ī, -īrī

　　Perfect: 4th principal part + esse

　　Future: future active participle + esse

Imperatives:

　　Singular: -āre, -ēre, -ere, -īre (looks like pres. act. inf.)

　　Plural: stem + -minī (same as 2nd person pl. pres. ind.)

Participles: Follows regular rules of forming participles

Ablative with Special Deponents

The ablative is used idiomatically with certain deponent verbs. An ablative is used as object of the following verbs:

1. ūtor (to use)
2. fruor (to enjoy)
3. fungor (to perform)
4. potior (to possess)
5. vēscor (to eat)

Chapter 36 Grammar

Irregular Verb
fīō, fierī, factus sum: *to occur, to happen, to be done, to be made*

Present Tense	Future Tense	Imperfect Tense	Subjuntive Present	Subjuntive Imperfect
fīō	fīam	fīēbam	fīam	fierem
fīs	fīēs	fīēbās	fīās	fierēs
fit	fīet	fīēbat	fīat	fieret
fīmus	fīēmus	fīēbāmus	fīāmus	fierēmus
fītis	fīētis	fīēbātis	fīātis	fierētis
fīunt	fīent	fīēbant	fīant	fierent

Infinitive	Imperative
fierī	Sg: fī, Pl: fīte

Used instead of the present system passive forms of faciō.

Chapter 37 Grammar
Conjugation of *Eō*

Irregular Verb: Eō, īre, iī, itum, *to go*

Indicative

Present	Future	Imperfect	Perfect	Future Perf.	Pluperfect
eō	ībō	ībam	iī	ierō	ieram
īs	ībis	ībās	īstī	ieris	ierās
it	ībit	ībat	iit	ierit	ierat
īmus	ībimus	ībāmus	iimus	ierimus	ierāmus
ītis	ībitis	ībātis	īstis	ieritis	ierātis
eunt	ībunt	ībant	iērunt	ierint	ierant

Subjunctive

Present	Imperfect	Perfect	Pluperfect
eam	īrem	ierim	īssem
eās	īrēs	ierīs	īssēs
eat	īret	ierit	īsset
eāmus	īrēmus	ierīmus	īssēmus
eātis	īrētis	ierītis	īssētis
eant	īrent	ierint	īssent

Imperative
Singular: ī
Plural: īte

Participles
Present: iēns
Future: itūrus, -a, -um

Infinitives
Present: īre
Future: itūrus esse
Perfect: īsse

Gerund
eundī

Chapter 38 Grammar
Supines

Supines for Model Verbs

Acc.	laudātum
Abl.	laudātū
Acc.	monitum
Abl.	monitū
Acc.	āctum
Abl.	āctū
Acc.	audītum
Abl.	audītū
Acc.	captum
Abl.	captū

The accusative indicates purpose with verbs of motion.

The ablative indicates in what respect a particular quality is applicable.

Chapter 39 Grammar
Gerund and Gerundives

Declension of Gerunds

Gen.	laudandī	dūcendī	sequendī	audiendī
Dat.	laudandō	dūcendō	sequendō	audiendō
Acc.	laudandum	dūcendum	sequendum	audiendum
Abl.	laudandō	dūcendō	sequendō	audiendō

Declension of Gerundives

Refer to future passive participle in Chapter 23.

Chapter 40 Grammar
Genitive and Ablative of Description; Direct Questions

Genitive and Ablative of Description

An ablative or genitive noun-adjective pair can be used to describe another noun.

Used for descriptions of character, quality, or size.

Direct Questions with *-Ne*, *Num*, and *Nōnne*

-ne suffixed to first word introduces a question.

nōnne: speaker expects "yes" answer

num: speaker expects "no" answer

Made in United States
North Haven, CT
24 September 2023